Sting Piano S...

Cover photo by Olaf Heine

ISBN 0-634-02515-5

7777 W. BLUEMOUND RD. P.O.BOX 13819 MILWAUKEE, WI 53213

For all works contained herein:
Unauthorized copying, arranging, adapting, recording or public performance is an infringement of copyright.
Infringers are liable under the law.

Visit Hal Leonard Online at
www.halleonard.com

4	ALL THIS TIME
10	BE STILL MY BEATING HEART
15	BRAND NEW DAY
22	DESERT ROSE
27	ENGLISHMAN IN NEW YORK
31	FIELDS OF GOLD
35	FORTRESS AROUND YOUR HEART
39	FRAGILE
43	IF YOU LOVE SOMEBODY SET THEM FREE
48	LOVE IS STRONGER THAN JUSTICE (THE MUNIFICENT SEVEN)
54	SHAPE OF MY HEART
58	THE SOUL CAGES
64	WE'LL BE TOGETHER
68	WHEN WE DANCE

All This Time

Written and Composed by G.M. Sumner

© 1991 STEERPIKE (OVERSEAS) LTD.
This arrangement © 2002 STEERPIKE (OVERSEAS) LTD.
Administered by MAGNETIC PUBLISHING LTD. (PRS) and EMI BLACKWOOD MUSIC INC. (BMI)
All Rights Reserved   International Copyright Secured   Used by Permission

Be Still My Beating Heart

Written and Composed by G.M. Sumner

© 1987 G.M. SUMNER
This arrangement © 2002 G.M. SUMNER
Administered by MAGNETIC PUBLISHING LTD. (PRS) and EMI BLACKWOOD MUSIC INC. (BMI)
All Rights Reserved   International Copyright Secured   Used by Permission

Brand New Day

Written and Composed by G.M. Sumner

© 1999 STEERPIKE (OVERSEAS) LTD.
This arrangement © 2002 STEERPIKE (OVERSEAS) LTD.
Administered by MAGNETIC PUBLISHING LTD. (PRS) and EMI BLACKWOOD MUSIC INC. (BMI)
All Rights Reserved   International Copyright Secured   Used by Permission

Desert Rose

Written and Composed by G.M. Sumner   Arabic Lyrics by Cheb Mami

Moderato ♩=108

© 1999 STEERPIKE (OVERSEAS) LTD. and DELABEL EDITIONS SARL
This arrangement © 2002 STEERPIKE (OVERSEAS) LTD. and DELABEL EDITIONS SARL
STEERPIKE (OVERSEAS) LTD. Administered by MAGNETIC PUBLISHING LTD. (PRS) and EMI BLACKWOOD MUSIC INC. (BMI)
DELABEL EDITIONS SARL Administered by EMI BLACKWOOD MUSIC INC. (BMI)
All Rights Reserved   International Copyright Secured   Used by Permission

Englishman in New York
Written and Composed by G.M. Sumner

© 1987 G.M. SUMNER
This arrangement © 2002 G.M. SUMNER
Administered by MAGNETIC PUBLISHING LTD. (PRS) and EMI Blackwood Music Inc. (BMI)
All Rights Reserved   International Copyright Secured   Used by Permission

Fields of Gold
Written and Composed by G.M. Sumner

© 1993 STEERPIKE LTD.
This arrangement © 2002 STEERPIKE LTD.
Administered by MAGNETIC PUBLISHING LTD. (PRS) and EMI BLACKWOOD MUSIC INC. (BMI)
All Rights Reserved   International Copyright Secured   Used by Permission

Fortress Around Your Heart

Written and Composed by G.M. Sumner

© 1985 G.M. SUMNER
This arrangement © 2002 G.M. SUMNER
Administered by MAGNETIC PUBLISHING LTD. (PRS) and EMI BLACKWOOD MUSIC INC. (BMI)
All Rights Reserved   International Copyright Secured   Used by Permission

Fragile

Written and Composed by G.M. Sumner

© 1987 G.M. SUMNER
This arrangement © 2002 G.M. SUMNER
Administered by MAGNETIC PUBLISHING LTD. (PRS) and EMI BLACKWOOD MUSIC INC. (BMI)
All Rights Reserved   International Copyright Secured   Used by Permission

If You Love Somebody Set Them Free

Written and Composed by G.M. Sumner

Fade Out

Love Is Stronger Than Justice
(The Munificent Seven)
Written and Composed by G.M. Sumner

© 1993 STEERPIKE LTD.
This arrangement © 2002 STEERPIKE LTD.
Administered by MAGNETIC PUBLISHING LTD. (PRS) and EMI BLACKWOOD MUSIC INC. (BMI)
All Rights Reserved   International Copyright Secured   Used by Permission

Fade Out

Shape of My Heart

Written and Composed by G.M. Sumner   Music by Dominic Miller

The Soul Cages
Written and Composed by G.M. Sumner

© 1991 STEERPIKE (OVERSEAS) LTD.
This arrangement © 2002 STEERPIKE (OVERSEAS) LTD.
Administered by MAGNETIC PUBLISHING LTD. (PRS) and EMI BLACKWOOD MUSIC INC. (BMI)
All Rights Reserved   International Copyright Secured   Used by Permission

We'll Be Together

Written and Composed by G.M. Sumner

© 1987 G.M. SUMNER
This arrangement © 2002 G.M. SUMNER
Administered by MAGNETIC PUBLISHING LTD. (PRS) and EMI BLACKWOOD MUSIC INC. (BMI)
All Rights Reserved   International Copyright Secured   Used by Permission

When We Dance

Written and Composed by G.M. Sumner

© 1994 STEERPIKE LTD.
This arrangement © 2002 STEERPIKE LTD.
Administered by MAGNETIC PUBLISHING LTD. (PRS) and EMI BLACKWOOD MUSIC INC. (BMI)
All Rights Reserved   International Copyright Secured   Used by Permission